Something
Beyond Me

God's Supernatural Divine Grace

Tina Releford

Something Beyond Me: God's Supernatural Divine Grace

Copyright © 2015 by Tina Releford

All rights reserved.

This book or any portion thereof may not be reproduced or used in any manner whatsoever without the express written permission of the author except for the use of brief quotations in a book review.

Cover Artwork by:
TYRO Publishing Services
http://www.tyropublishing.com

For inquiries please contact the author in writing:

Printed in the United States of America First Printing, 2015

ISBN-13: 978-069-2633-62-5

ISBN-10: 0692633626

TYRO Publishing Services

Dedication

In loving memory of my husband...

Pastor Michael Releford
Feb. 19, 1959-Dec. 20, 2014

This book is dedicated to the late *Pastor Michael Releford*, who was the love of my life, my husband, Pastor, best friend and my soul mate. He was an anointed and mighty man of God, who truly loved the Lord. He believed in God, the God in me, and was my biggest motivator and supporter. When he told me everything was going to be alright, I believed him, because he had great faith in God. Michael enjoyed being a Pastor, and he truly had a Pastor's heart. He wanted everyone that he came in contact with to fall in love with the God that he served and loved. Michael was very passionate about prayer, and the fact that prayer changes things and if you pray long enough, prayer would change you. He was a loving husband, father, grandfather, and brother. Furthermore, Michael had a very forgiving and loving spirit toward all.

My hope is that this book will be a blessing and give hope to whomever hands it comes in contact with. I do know one thing for sure that it was **Something Beyond Me** that brought me through my tragedy; it was ***God's Supernatural Divine Grace!***

Jesus said unto her, I am the resurrection, and the life: he that believeth in me, though he were dead, yet shall he live:

John 11:25 (KJV)

Table of Contents

Dedication   *3*
Acknowledgments   *7*

My Prayer	12
Transitioning from Wife to Widow	13
Transitioning from Co-Pastor to Pastor	22
Five Stages of Grief by Elisabeth Kübler Ross	25
Transitioning from Weakness to Sufficient Grace	28
Transition from Depression to Exuberance	40
Transition from Grace to Grace	44
Transition from Grief to Hope	52
Pastor Releford Inspiring Quotes	58
About the Author	*60*

Acknowledgments

I thank God for all his amazing grace, favor and His many blessings. I am so humbled and grateful to Him for all that He has done for me and in me. I'm grateful for an ear to hear as the Holy Spirit Directed me to write. Thank you God for waking up one of the many books that is on the inside of me.

To my Parents: The late Mr. Belvin & Mrs. Opal Perry, although I lost them at a very early age, yet I have not forgotten all the love and the teaching they both instilled in me. Love is one of the most important things that they taught me.

To my children: Thank you for always believing in me and for your love and continuing support: Antonio & Shameka Dixon, Tony & Annitra Jones, Michelle Releford, Kendell & Nikki Releford, and all my grandchildren, I love you all dearly.

My siblings: Thank you for all of your prayers, love and support and standing by my side, and allowing me to lean on you and draw strength from each one of you.

My God-Mother: Ms. Margaret Parker, May God Bless you, for stepping in and supporting and loving me.

My Apostle -Trixie Morgan: for speaking powerful motivating words in my life and for all the prayers. For pushing me and giving me everything that is always on the inside of you, just like you said you were going to do.

All the prayer warriors, family members and church family and my dear friends that stood in the gap for me.

I would first like to say how proud I am of this great Woman of God in the hardest Season of her life that she sought the face of God and stayed focused to write this AWESOME book. Prophetess Tina Releford loves The Lord and she loves his people. She is a part of what God is doing in this season through this Great Woman. Prophetess Tina has pioneered and paved the way for many young women to follow. She is full of life, full of wisdom and her ministry reaches beyond racial and denomination and gender barriers.

A Conference host, Author, Teacher, Preacher and Prophet. I am honored to be a mentor and a spiritual covering for her. My prayer is that God will continue to do great things in her life that she will reach the multitude through her writing and preaching. Love you so much. May God continue to supply and meet every one of your needs.

Apostle Trixie Morgan

Blessing in Abundance,

Greetings, In the name of our Lord and Savior Jesus Christ. It is with great honor, admiration, and respect that I proclaim Blessings in Abundance upon my beloved sister, and awesome woman of God, Prophetess Tina Releford. I pray Blessing in Abundance upon her that this book will meet and exceed her Spiritual as well as her financial expectations. Also I pray Blessing in Abundance upon you the readers and receivers of her Spiritual words from an awesome God that we serve that will Bless, Enhance, Inspire and move you forward in your spiritual walk with God. Blessing in Abundance to Prophetess Tina Releford, In the name of Jesus Christ..... Amen.

Reverend Gary O. Perry

I address this paragraph "To whom it may concern" because I believe that this testament of my prayer request to God asking him for a friend, and in asking I was specific as to what type of friend I needed. God answered my prayer quickly and connected me with the late great Pastor Mike Releford of Spirit to Spirit Ministries Inc. Our friendship grew into a brotherhood , Pastor Mike was a man who believed God and love to pray, a great servant unto the people of God, a great husband to his wife Prophetess Tina and great father to all his children and grandchildren. One of the many special qualities he possess was the ability to sacrifice time to laugh with Griffin, Pastor Mike was just special like that, whenever you needed him he was there, for I am grateful that I was blessed to have Pastor Mike as my friend and brother, for his presence is greatly missed. I bid him a great farewell, for I can hear him shouting all the way in heaven this one word **"GLORY"**!!!!!!!!

Pastor Xavier L Griffin Sr.

To our Mother: We are so very proud to be your children. We are proud of the things you have accomplished. We have always admired your strength and even more than that, your faith. Growing up we often wondered how you could be strong. Even when it seemed things were difficult we never saw you lose faith. As a teenager we wondered where is she getting "this" from? As a woman, mother, and a wife, and because of your example we know where your help comes from. Being a Parent now we realize what a big responsibility that is. We realize that it's a tough job yet so rewarding. We understand the worry and the prayers and the wanting the best for us. We understand. We get it. We are thankful to God that we had a mother that worried about us but most of all that prayed for us and still prays for us. We're just godly proud that you are our mother. I think it's safe to say that you can look at us now and know that you did a good job. You've been through so much throughout your life, but look at you now-still standing in God's grace and His love. You are such an awesome woman, mother, friend, Gi-Gi, Prophetess, and inspiration. You are just awesome and we love you to life!!!!

"On behalf of your children"

My Prayer

Dear Heavenly Father, The God that can do immeasurably more than we could ever think or imagine. I pray that the person that is reading this book will get to experience you like they have never experience you before. I ask you God, to extend to them the same Sufficient Grace that you extend to me during my season of grief. Heavenly Father, I pray that you would release Grace over them through the Power of the Holy Spirit, which will enable them to do what they could never do on their own, in Jesus name. I pray that they receive your grace which can only be received through faith, and that they will begin to live by faith, through grace. I pray that they will begin to walk in a **Hebrew 11:1 "Now Faith"**, and even in their time of weakness they will come to believe that you God are still able to work your divine plan through them, because when they are weak, yet you are strong. I pray that they will receive wisdom to understand that whatever they need to do today, that if they will lean on you God and let you empower them with a Fresh Supernatural Divine Grace...In Jesus Name!!!!

Prophetess Tina Releford

Transitioning from Wife to Widow

On December 20 2014, I was on my way to a funeral with my Pastor who was also my husband (Pastor Michael Releford). My husband was going to do the Eulogy at a home going service at 11 a.m. that morning. We got up and got ready as we always did when we would go to do a funeral, or any other assignment or preaching engagement. Pastor Releford would always pray and seek the Lord for the instructions for all his assignments, as to what God wanted him to say to the people of God. Whenever Pastor Releford, had an assignment he was very quiet, which was not unusual for him before an assignment. He took his call and assignments very seriously. The house had to be very quiet, and he did not like to be disturbed, and I respected that and gave him his space. He was very serious about his meditation time and his private time with God. He would meditate and pray, I would pray, and then we would pray together. We did all the things that a pastor and co-pastor would do to prepare before a service or assignment. Every Sunday morning, his best friend would always call him and the two of them would have prayer together. They would have a pep talk and a mini sermon; they would basically have church, before church. They were always there to encourage each other in that way.

On our way to eulogize his cousin's home-going celebration service, we had a conversation about an upcoming ministry trip. We were invited to be the guest speakers at a Sweetheart Retreat in Cedartown Georgia, the weekend after Valentine's Day. We began to discuss some plans about the trip and we were very excited about the opportunity to go and minister to married couples about keeping GOD, LOVE and ROMANCE in a marriage. I remember his face just light up as we were having this discussion. Michael and I loved to minister and share with other people how God had truly blessed our marriage.

My husband began to preach to the congregation about *"Finding Jesus at a Time of Grief"*, without a sign, signal, or warning, right in the mist of the eulogy my husband- collapsed while releasing God's Words of comfort to the family and passes away. My husband made his transition while preaching the word of God.

Pastor Releford read the scripture from the book of *John 11:25* (KJV) *Jesus said unto her, I am the*

resurrection, and the life: he that believeth in me, though he was dead, yet shall he live:
On the front of the Home-going celebration program of the deceased, which he was doing the eulogy for was this scripture, *John 13:7* (NLV) *Jesus answered him, "You do not understand now what I am doing but you will later."*

Pastor Releford always took great joy in having the opportunity to minister to his family. He had such a strong burden for his family and wanted them to have a relationship with the same God that he loved and served. He loved his family and everyone that he came in contact with. He was always in a very exciting mood, but always a serious mood and stayed focus on the assignment. He loved serving the Lord. Pastor Releford was so excited, about the message that God had given him to share, in the hope that someone would accept Jesus as their Lord and Savior. While he was exhorting God, someone's phone rang and he made the statement; "If that is not Jesus you better not answer it, because I've got something to say." Then, Pastor continued sharing with the family and friends about *"Finding Jesus in a Time of Grief."* One of Pastor Releford's strongest point in his message was to always inform the people of God whether they were saved or unsaved, that heaven is a prepared place for prepared people. He was also informing them to get ready and stay ready for Jesus' return, because we don't know when Jesus will come. Next, he ended that statement with "God is good!" And those were his last and final words.

Pastor Releford collapsed and fell straight backwards. I thought he had got too hot and just fainted, but something felt wrong, totally wrong. People gathering around to see what was going on and I asked them to get back and just start praying. There was a nurse and a Fire Chief there to assist him until the EMS arrived. There were several women who gathered around me to help keep me calm. I began to pray and continue to pray and called on Jesus for comfort and strength. I tried to remain hopeful, but it was so hard, because he never got back up. I felt in my heart that he had expired, but I continued to hope and pray.

John 13:7 (NLV), Jesus answered him, "You do not understand now what I am doing but you will later." The way my husband's transition took place, was so hard for many to understand, including myself. There were so many unanswered questions, as how he transitioned during the middle of eulogizing his cousin's home-going celebration. Michael had not been sick nor did he make any complaints of not feeling well or tired that morning. He was not the type to complain about to much of anything but would pray about everything as the scripture would say. *Philippians 4:6(NLT) Don't worry about anything;*

instead, pray about everything. Tell God what you need, and thank him for all he has done. Pastor Releford loved to pray, and believed in the power of prayer. Prayer joins the heart of people on earth with the heart of God in heaven.

Everyone was trying to figure out what God was doing or what was the message or statement that God was making. *John 13:7, You do not understand now what I am doing but you will later & John 11:25 (KJV) Jesus said unto her, I am the resurrection, and the life: he that believeth in me, though he were dead, yet shall he live:* was the two scriptures that God tied together for his divine message that day. God was really sending out a very powerful message to those that had an ear to hear.

But who can know the mind of Christ (1Corinthians 2:16). Who would ever be able to figure out our God? The God with an infinite mind, who is limited or endless in space, that is impossible to measure or calculate. If we could ever figure out God and if we always knew what God was thinking or planning. If we knew all the answers to all the when's, where's and why's and how's; then we wouldn't need a God. We'll never be able to out think or figure out God with our finite minds. We as a people have limits and a finite amount of memory. When things catch us by surprise, it doesn't catch God by surprise. We have to have a Spiritual mind to be able to comprehend the spiritual things of God. It is not our responsibility to try and figure out God or to out think God, but it's our responsibility and an opportunity to get to know Him and to make Him known. Trying to out think God is impossible. Therefore we have to have a relationship with Him to understand the spiritual things. Building a relationship with God, and having an understanding of who He is, is very possible. *Isaiah 55:8 (KJV), For my thoughts are not your thoughts, neither are your ways my ways, saith the Lord.* In due seasons he reveals to us what we need to know at the appointed time of maturity.

The Bible *says in Mark 13:32-33*, "But of that day or hour no one knows, not even the angels in heaven, nor the Son, but the Father alone. *Take heed keep on the alert; for you do not know when the appointed time will come.*" We should pay very close attention to this scripture. My husband lived a holy and righteous life and God had a greater need for him in Glory. He lived his life in preparation of living an eternal life with God. No one knows the day or hour nor do we know when our appointed time is. If God can remove a righteous man while in the mist of his assignment, then what is that saying to the rest of the world and what is it saying to the Church? We need to be ready, so that we can spend eternity in Heaven with God and not in Hell. Heaven is a prepared place for prepared people. *John 14:2-3, (KJV) In my Father's house are many mansions:*

if it were not so, I would have told you. I go to prepare a place for you. And if I go and prepare a place for you, I will come again, and receive you unto myself; that where I am, there ye may be also.

Pastor Releford was a man who truly loved the Lord. *He was a man after God's own heart. It did not take a lot of discussion about God to get him hype and excited.* He loved preaching, teaching and talking about the goodness of Jesus. Pastor Releford walked with God; he was a type of Enoch and he was a type of Elijah. There were many that saw him transition. He always said when it was his time, he was going to go up as though he was going up in the rapture. The bible says in *2 Corinthians 5:8 (KJV), "We are confident, I say, and willing rather to be absent from the body, and to be present with the Lord."* I knew that he was absent in the body and in the presence of the Lord, giving me somewhat of a peace.

This was by far one of the hardest and longest days of my life. I was so very confused and trying to figure out what just happen. I tried my best to remain positive and to remain hopeful. I did not know and understand what I just witnessed, but as painful and as hard as it was, I had just witnessed my husband transition, while doing what he loved doing the most; **PREACHING**, preaching about Jesus; in whom you can find hope in the mist of despair. **Wow!!!**

I have peace and joy knowing without a doubt that his transition and destination was heaven bound and I have joy in knowing that his transition got a lot of people's attention as he ministered to the saved and unsaved. This was a supernatural demonstration of God's divine power that they will never forget and never stop talking about, and this powerful demonstration will not be in vain. This really got a lot of people's attention and opened many eyes.

Many made the statement:
- "I really need to change my way of life."
- "I have got to build a better relationship with God."
- "No one is exempt from death, no matter what type of life that they live."
- "I have got to do better."

God put something on their mind and on their heart. *Matthew 24:42 (NLT), So you, too, must keep watch! For we don't know what day God is coming. Therefore we need to be alert, be constant on the alert. Keep your eyes open. Keep wide awake!* Being watchful means to live a sanctified life; consciously aware of the coming judgment day. The just shall live by faith in Jesus Christ, looking forward to the coming of the Bridegroom and King.

When I mention **"Something Beyond Me"**; that something beyond me was **God's Supernatural**

Divine Grace. Here I was a Pastor Wife/Co Pastor/Prophetess of Spirit to Spirit Ministries, just recently ordain on June 22, 2013. This ministry began as an outreach, which processed into a church that we started in the living room of our home. We later out grew our living room and had to move to a conference room at a local motel. We then moved to the building that we reside in today. A wife, mother, grandmother—to a Widow, to carry this Infant Ministry without my husband; how was I going to do this? We did pretty much everything together, but still the ministry must continue on. I had to move forward and continue the work of the ministry. I knew he would have wanted me to continue and declare the works of the Lord as the scripture say in Psalm 118:17 (KJV), I shall not die, but live, and declare the works of the Lord.

Transitioning from Co-Pastor to Pastor

I truly did not want to continue this ministry without my husband. I began to pray and ask the Lord how I could continue to declare the works and grieve for my husband at the same time. The bible says in *Mark 10:8 (NKJV), and the two shall become one flesh'; so then they are no longer two, but one flesh.* We were truly one "Spirit to Spirit" *and how can two walk together except they agree.* We always tried to walk together in agreement, because we understood that there is power in agreement.

I felt the separation when he transition, and I didn't think I could carry the weight of the ministry without my husband. Pastor Releford was so strong and wise in the Lord. The Holy Ghost brought things back to my remembrance, that I may be temporarily separated from my husband and I would see him again someday. I had to also be reminded that the Holy Spirit continues to dwell in me and *that I can do all things through Jesus Christ who strengthens me,* God will give me grace, strength and the power that I need to continue on. (Something Beyond Me)

I had lost the love of my life, my best friend, my soul mate. The man that knew me inside and out, who was a good husband and provider that loved me unconditionally, loved his children, grandchildren, and family. A man who had a lifestyle based and built on prayer. He would always say that "prayer" changes things and if you pray long enough "prayer" will change you. I started to think and wonder how was I going to get through this? I knew that my husband would want me to carry on the ministry and to continue the work of the Lord. *JOHN 10:25 (KJV) says, "Jesus answered them, I told you, and ye believed not: the works that I do in my Father's name, they bear witness of me."* Let the work Pastor Releford did continue to speak for him. Michael was a pioneer and I did not want the legacy, the hard work, and the plowing that he had already started to end, so therefore I knew I had to continue on—*There was something beyond me!* I still grieve over the loss of my husband every day, but even in my weakest time I could still feel something that was much more powerful beyond me. So I pressed on. It was not easy, but I had to believe in my faith and trust God to take me through.

I wanted to share with you a chart of the *Five Stages of Grief* according to *Elisabeth Kubler Ross*, that I hope this will be beneficial to you or perhaps to someone else. This will also help you to comprehend what level someone else may be experiencing during their time of grief. We have to also remember no two people grieve the same. I can truly say I found myself in some of these areas, but through it all, I had to keep trusting and believing in my faith in God that He would bring me through this process. *God's Supernatural Divine Grace* had become a very important indwelling quality within me.

Five Stages of Grief by Elisabeth Kübler Ross

1 - Denial
Denial is a conscious or unconscious refusal to accept facts, information, reality, etc., relating to the situation concerned. It's a defense mechanism and perfectly natural. Some people can become locked in this stage when dealing with a traumatic change that can be ignored. Death of course is not particularly easy to avoid or evade indefinitely.

2 - Anger
Anger can manifest in different ways. People dealing with emotional upset can be angry with themselves, and/or with others, especially those close to them. Knowing this helps keep detached and non-judgmental when experiencing the anger of someone who is very upset.

3 - Bargaining
Traditionally the bargaining stage for people facing death can involve attempting to bargain with God or

whatever the person believes in. People facing less serious trauma can bargain or seek to negotiate a compromise. For example "Can we still be friends?" when facing a break-up. Bargaining rarely provides a sustainable solution, especially if it's a matter of life or death.

4 - Depression
Also referred to as preparatory grieving. In a way it's the dress rehearsal or the practice run for the 'aftermath' although this stage means different things depending on whom it involves. It's a sort of acceptance with emotional attachment. It's natural to feel sadness and regret, fear, uncertainty, etc. It shows that the person has at least begun to accept the reality.

5 - Acceptance
Again this stage definitely varies according to the person's situation, although broadly it is an indication that there is some emotional detachment and objectivity. People dying can enter this stage a long time before the people they leave behind, who must necessarily pass through their own individual stages of dealing with the grief.

I remember on December 27th, 11 am, the day of my husband home going celebration, I wanted to say something at the service but didn't know if I would be strong enough to stand, walk, or talk without breaking down. I was so weak. The night before the home going service we had a memorial service with the theme "Sooner Night" my husband loved OU Sooners. Everyone was asked to wear OU shirts, hats, etc. There were so many people there, which let me know the strong impact that my husband had on so many people lives. Before dismissing I had the last words. I thank everyone for coming and wanted to encourage the people to ask God to help them to be better today than you were on yesterday. Pastor Releford always would say these words. He would look at himself in the mirror from time to time and he would speak to the man in the mirror and say, "I am not satisfied with that man in the mirror." Those words always challenged and encouraged him to be better and to do better today than what he was or did on yesterday. He set a goal to become a better Man.

Transitioning from Weakness to Sufficient Grace

The morning of my husband's home-going celebration, as I step into the pulpit with the assistance of two of my brothers, I looked out and saw hundreds of people, some were sitting and some standing; once again there was a strong impact. I thought to myself, *what do I say or do now Lord?* I took a deep breath (breathe in) and it felt like I received power that was beyond me, *something that was beyond me.* I felt as if I was inflated by a *something that was beyond me.* I receive power and strength that was beyond me. *In Ephesians 3:16 (KJV)* Paul prayed to God for the Ephesians that God *would grant them, according to the riches of his glory, to be strengthened with might by his Spirit in their inner man.* I felt that same way, someone had to have been praying for me as well. I then asked God to give me the strength to do or say what I needed to say. God answered by doing something that was beyond my own natural strength. I was just a willing vessel, obedient enough to be used by God and to step out of myself, and move out of Gods way to allow Him to take control. It truly was a supernatural divine power of grace, which was beyond me.

The Holy Spirit blew up on the inside of me as though God breathed something in me that was beyond me. What I breathed in came back out to be God's powerful anointing in words. I felt my weak frail body being inflated with power beyond me. I felt something stirring and moving inside that came from beyond me. *God's Supernatural Divine Grace* was being manifested right before the very eyes of His people throughout the room. The Bible says in *2 Cor. 12*:9, *"My grace is sufficient for you, for my power is made perfect in weakness. Therefore I will boast all the more gladly about my weaknesses, so that Christ's power may rest on you."* This scripture is the true meaning of God's *"Sustaining Sufficient Grace,"* which is available no matter what the struggle is. It is enough to see us through every trial we face. When I open my mouth powerful words came out and God's Supernatural Divine Grace stepped up.

God will also give us *"Serving Grace"* which is God's resources and power to do all we need to do for Him. *Ephesians 3:7-8 (AMP), Of this [Gospel] I was made a minister according to the gift of God's free grace (undeserved favor) which was bestowed on me by the exercise (the working in all its effectiveness) of His power. To me, though I am the very least of all the saints (God's consecrated people), this grace (favor, privilege) was granted and graciously entrusted: to proclaim to the Gentiles the unending (boundless, fathomless, incalculable, and exhaustless) riches of Christ [wealth which no human being could have searched out].*

According to *Wikipedia*, Divine grace is a theological term, which is defined as the divine influence which operates in humans to regenerate and sanctify, to inspire virtuous impulses, and to impart strength to endure trial and resist temptation.

As I was thinking and praying about what to say at my husband home-going celebration, *Psalms 13* kept coming to my spirit. I thought about how David expressed his frustration, abandonment and anger in his time of distress. David felt God had walked away from him and in his situation and that God couldn't be found. David grieves over his situation; he had to know that hope comes from God. There are times when we go through unexpected tragedy or distress, we feel as though God has left us or does not hear us or see us. The answer to God's delay is to trust in His loving kindness and to remember that in the past he was there for us in His timing and way. At the end of *Palms 13* David ends with these words: *Psalms 13:5-6, But I have trusted in Your loving-kindness; My heart shall rejoice in Your salvation. I will sing to the Lord, because He has dealt bountifully with me.* When we go back and read God's Word it will give us that assurance that we need that will help us to remember that he is a faithful God. We must remember to trust the timing of God and that He is not a God that will tell a lie. *Numbers 23:19 (NIV), God is not human, that he should lie, not a human being, that he should change his mind. Does he speak and then not act? Does he promise and not fulfill?*

I don't clearly remember everything that I said to the congregation, but there was one important thing that stuck out in my spirit and I hope was imparted into many of their spirits. The Holy Ghost spoke to the people and said; "We are people that live in a why world, and we should get to know the "WHO"". I would admit that I ask God the entire "Why" questions I could think of: why me, why my husband, and why now. God spoke and said not WHY...but WHO. Not to ask why, but get to know the WHO. Get to know the WHO, which is in control of all of your circumstances. Stop focusing on the why and build a relationship with the WHO, the one who is the maker and created and the one that is in control of every aspect in our lives. At that particular moment, God was my strength, comforter and my peace.

Proverbs 3:5 (KJV), Trust in the Lord with all thine heart; and lean not unto thine own understanding.

I had to just keep reflecting on WHO God is. Over the years and in this particular season of my life, I have truly gotten to experience some of the many different names of God, and He is truly amazing.

I have read many different definitions of Grace. The Apostle Paul began many of his letters with the phrase, *Grace and peace to you from God our Father and the Lord Jesus Christ (Romans 1:7; Ephesians 1:2; 1 Corinthians 1:3).* God is the instigator of grace, and it is from Him that all other grace flows. The whole movement, every shift, everything we do in our life from beginning to end is dependent on God's grace. Grace can be easily remembered by this simple acrostic: **G**od's **R**iches **A**t **C**hrist's **E**xpense. Grace is simple elegance or refinement of movement. The bible translated g*race* in the New Testament comes from the Greek word charis, which means favor, blessing, or kindness. When the word grace is used in connection with God, it takes on a more powerful meaning. Grace is God choosing to bless us rather than curse us as our sin deserves. Grace, which is accessed only by faith, according to *Wikipedia*, is also the power of God by which He does righteousness through anyone who will yield to Him. In my opinion grace is the quality of high standard of EXCELLENCE.

There are also many different types of grace that we receive from God: saving grace, sustaining, sufficient grace, and serving grace; that most of us have experienced.

There was days when I did not want to go anywhere and days when I did not want to get up out of bed. I did a lot of crying but this scripture was so comforting to me, *Psalm 56:8 (NLT) You keep track of all my sorrows. You have collected all my tears in your bottle. You have recorded each one in your book.* God was aware of every tear that I shed and every hurt and pain that I endured. I had a lot of sleepless nights and some uncomfortable and lonely days. I miss my husband. The love that he and I share was awesome. We did not have a perfect marriage, but we had a blessed marriage and friendship, and that is all because of our love for God and the relationship we had with Him. I thank God for the years that we shared together and I was very blessed to be his wife and friend.

The first two weeks following my husband's passing were difficult, not to mention that he passed away 3 days before our wedding anniversary and 5 days before Christmas. The nights were long and restless. It felt terrible. Thankfully, I have some powerful women in my life that I was able to call to pray me through those most difficult moments. My youngest daughter stayed with me during those first two weeks. She was there in the middle of the night when I would wake up crying. She held me. She prayed for me, while I cried. It was as if she was the mother and I was the child. I realize now that God had to wake me up to let me know this release was an important part of my process. There were some family members and close friends that slept over for almost two months so that I would not have to grieve alone. When I began to gain strength I knew it was time for me to release them. It was important that I continue through the process of healing on my own.

When I would go out to eat or go to the store or take care of my personal business, or out to a simple place like a basketball game, which I love, I felt as though people treated me different. Some people would stare, some would not speak, and some people's mouth would just drop open. Sometimes people seem to feel uncomfortable around me, wondering what to say or what to do and this made me feel very uncomfortable too. I became very annoyed and frustrated. I was wondering if I was not supposed to enjoy life anymore, laugh or smile ever again. The Bible says in *Nehemiah 8:10 (NIV "...The joy of the LORD is your strength."* So some of the things that I liked doing that brought me joy and helped me to smile, I did. God was always in the central of everything I did. He was truly my strength.

I had thought about not ever leaving my house again. I got caught up in my feelings and my flesh. At home

I felt safe and secure and I didn't have to experience that feeling again. Each time I would go somewhere this happen for a brief moment. I didn't want to become bitter, angry or upset with anyone. I believe if something is making us feel some type of way, we need to take to the Lord in prayer, so that God can minister to us and give us direction, so I prayed. I remember praying and asking God what was going on, and why am I feeling like this. God's answer to me was; "First, this is not about you." "Second, but it is all about *"Something Beyond You."* God spoke to me and said, "I'm going to use you to demonstrate to my people and show them "This Is What Grace Looks Like." When you think the people are looking at you they are actually looking at my *Supernatural Divine Grace* being manifested all over you and through you. There will be another widow that will need to see my divine grace; there will be another parent or pastor that will need to see what my divine grace looks like. There will even be the saved and unsaved that will need to comprehend, understand, and gain revelation of the scripture. *Ephesians 2:8 says, "For by grace are you saved, through faith, and that not of yourselves. The only way any of us can enter into a relationship with God is because of His grace toward us."*

The more grace God released to me, the more I began to understand His grace. In faith, I began to walk in a new grace. Each day I would ask God for His grace and thank him for it. God's grace is so refreshing. God breathes something (GRACE) in me that was beyond me. I began not to allow my feelings to be in control of my day. I learn to live beyond my feelings. I learn to walk in the power of thankfulness which releases God's grace. We can learn to manage our emotions rather than allowing them to manage us. No matter what our current situation is, we still have something to be thankful for. God's grace will be sufficient each day to help us survive and live out the full measure of life that God has ordained; and that through his grace you will complete your mission. I know that I cannot do anything without God's Grace.

Through this situation I'm really getting to see the manifestation of standing on the word and on God's promises. His Word and His promises will elevate you. *Hebrews 10:23 (KJV), Let us hold fast the profession of our faith without wavering; (for he is faithful that promised).*

According to *Wikipedia*, grace can also be the empowering presence of God enabling us to be who he created us to be, and to do what He has called us to do; the working power of God Himself. I have been given a new knowledge, wisdom and revelation as to how to go through my afflictions, trials, and tribulations. *James 1:5 (MSG) If you don't know what you're doing, pray to the Father. He loves to help. You'll get his help, and won't be condescended to when you ask for it. Ask boldly, believingly, without a second thought.*

Ask God for wisdom, which is instruction that only God can give us so that we will *know-how* to do things according to His ways. *Proverbs 2:6 (KJV) For the LORD giveth wisdom: out of his mouth cometh knowledge and understanding.* Wisdom is based upon knowledge. Often wisdom and knowledge are mentioned together, because wisdom can't exist without knowledge. Knowledge comes from the spiritual education (reading of God's Word), understanding and being able to comprehend God's Word. We need wisdom so that we will know how to apply God's Word (knowledge) to our problems and our life; wisdom to deal with situations and wisdom to know how to handle our afflictions, trials and tribulations. We have got to have the wisdom of God to *know-how* to apply the knowledge (God's Word) we have gain. Wisdom is not just knowledge but it's *knowing–how.* Wisdom is the skillfulness to formulate a plan and to carry it out in the best and most effective way. Ask God for His wisdom so that our decision will lead us to maturity and completeness.

As God began to enlarge my territory, and the doors began to open, I begin to ask myself the question, "Was I ready?" "Had I allowed myself enough time to grieve and heal?" This new place that I was walking in now was the greatest definition of what grace really was to me. This was God's way of demonstrating the very thing that was operating within me, that was beyond me. God divine supernatural grace, was what was helping me to keep it moving in my time of grief. I allow myself to decrease and God increased in me. I learn how to move out of God's way and give Him the right of way, I knew when to shift and let the Holy Ghost have total control. I was still very weak, but God gave me the strength. I allow Him to become greater in me than He had ever been before. That something that was beyond me was the power of God that was operating in me and through me in a totally different capacity and dimension. His grace is sufficient. So now when I think of the **IS** in the scripture, **2 Cor. 12:9, My grace "IS" sufficient,** it helps me to remember that I don't have to wait on God's grace, His amazing grace **IS** already sufficient and is available now, it's already here, just as soon as I ask for it. I don't have to wait for tomorrow's grace, I don't have to rely on the Grace of yesterday, and I can depend on His Grace right now! His Word tell us His grace is sufficient, right at the very moment that you cry out to God for grace, it is available for us.

You have to remember that my husband's eulogy topic at the home-going celebration that he preaching at was, *Finding Jesus in a Time of Grief.* I never lost Jesus, but I did get to experience Him in a greater capacity. I began to allow God to use me to display His Supernatural Divine Grace through me. Allowing God to use me to help someone else to find and tap into His grace, was a blessing for me. Grace is that supernatural strength we need to keep moving forward when we don't feel like it or we may be too weak to do so because of unexpected circumstances that may be out of our control.

Supernatural, according to *Wiktionary,* is above nature; that which is beyond or added to nature, often so considered because it is given by a deity or some force beyond that which humans are born with and the *Your Dictionary* states that supernatural is extraordinary or something associated with forces we don't understand or cannot explain by science, simply meaning that it is something beyond us that we cannot do our self. Only God can do the supernatural.

So when we go back and gather all the definitions together: *Supernatural, Divine*, and *Grace* and compound them together, it is simply, "The power of the Holy Spirit coming to us freely, enabling us to do for God, what we could never do on our own." The Bible Says in *Proverbs 4:7 (KJV), Wisdom is the principal thing; therefore get wisdom: and with all thy getting get understanding.* It is so important for us to understand God's Word.

Transition from Depression to Exuberance

Throughout this season, day by day when I ask God for grace, he released to me everything that I needed at that particular time. Grace is favor, and the strength that I needed to get up out of bed and to help me keep it moving. I thank God for his grace and His unconditional love. It was going to take God's grace for me to continue to walk out his will. There is the old saying that *"The will of God will not take you where the grace of God will not protect you."* I knew at that point and believed that I was walking in a new place of Grace, and that God was using me to show other widows, women, pastor, parents etc. what grace looks like. I knew that this was all of God's grace and nothing that I did myself and all the glory belongs to him because without him I could not walk in this place of this new grace. There was a point of time in that season that I begin to battle with depression. According to the chart from *Elisabeth Kübler Ross- - Five Stages of Grief*, I was on the fourth stage, so I ask God for His grace and His strength to fight the Spirit of depression. I refuse to be depressed, bitter and hopeless and it was *"Something Beyond Me"* that helped me to continue to keep moving forward.

Psalm 91:1 (KJV), Let me know that if I dwell in the secret place of the Most High, I could abide under the shadow of the Almighty. I choose to dwell and I decided to fight depression. Doctors often offer medication in order to treat the illness, but I choose to fight. The physical symptoms of depression include; sadness, emptiness, withdrawal from others, irritability, emotional sensitivity, low motivation and self-esteem, and suicidal thoughts (to name a few). Depression is also heaviness, burden, and sorrow or something hard to endure. Exuberance is the quality of being full of energy, excitement, and cheerfulness; ebullience, lively, high-spirited.

I began to find scriptures that would help me with my battle of depression. Depression is a Spirit, and it must be fought with the word of God and not medication. I fought back by praying and speaking the word of God over myself. Here is a list of scriptures that I would like to share with you:

- *Psalm 40:1-3* (KJV) *I waited patiently for the Lord; and he inclined unto me, and heard my cry. 2 He brought me up also out of an horrible pit, out of the miry clay, and set my feet upon a rock, and established my goings. 3 And he hath put a new song in my mouth, even praise unto our God: many shall see it, and fear, and shall trust in the Lord.*

- *Psalm 34:17-19 (KJV) 17 The righteous cry, and the Lord heareth, and delivereth them out of all their troubles. 18 The Lord is nigh unto them that are of a broken heart; and saveth such as be of a contrite spirit. 19 Many are the afflictions of the righteous: but the Lord delivereth him out of them all.*
- *Psalm 9:9 (KJV) The Lord also will be a refuge for the oppressed, a refuge in times of trouble.*
- *Psalm 55:22 (KJV) Cast thy burden upon the Lord, and he shall sustain thee: he shall never suffer the righteous to be moved.*
- *Deuteronomy 31:8 (KJV) And the Lord, he it is that doth go before thee; he will be with thee, he will not fail thee, neither forsake thee: fear not, neither be dismayed.*
- *Psalm 27:4-5 (KJV) One thing have I desired of the Lord, that will I seek after; that I may dwell in the house of the Lord all the days of my life, to behold the beauty of the Lord, and to enquire in his temple. 5 For in the time of trouble he shall hide me in his pavilion: in the secret of his tabernacle shall he hide me; he shall set me up upon a rock.*
- *2 Samuel 22:29 (KJV) – You are my lamp O Lord; the Lord turns my darkness into light.*

❖ *Psalm 126:5 (KJV) – Those who sow in tears will reap with songs of joy.*

I made a copy of the scriptures listed above, and put it by my bed and in other places in my house where I could see them. I was determined not to allow the Spirit of depression to have control over me. I didn't have any time in my life for the Spirit of depression nor was their room for the Spirit of depression in my home. I continued to pray and read and rebuke that Spirit of depression and ask God to give me more grace. The reading of the word of God brought some exuberance, which was the excitement, and cheerfulness that I needed. This really lifted my spirits.

Transition from Grace to Grace

I continued to pray and read and rebuke that Spirit of depression and ask God to give me more grace. Each time God extends grace, the new grace is greater than the previous grace. *John 1:16 (NIV), Out of his fullness we have all received grace in the place of grace already given.* One gracious gift after another, grace for grace, as long as we keep asking for it, and living right, we'll have it. It won't run out!

The Amplified Version records it this way, *John 1:16 (AMP),*[16] *For out of His fullness (abundance) we have all received [all had a share and we were all supplied with] one grace after another and spiritual blessing upon spiritual blessing and even favor upon favor and gift [heaped] upon gift.*

The more we live by grace, the more grace we have by which to live. The more grace we use, the more grace we have available. We never run out. In exchange for grace, we get more grace. There is no limit to God's grace. We will greatly be supplied with the grace of God. The supply is new every morning. The fountain from which the grace of God flows is an eternal fountain, it will never run out, and it will never run dry.

We need God's grace, we can't live without it. God's grace cannot be purchased and we cannot earn it. It only comes by means of a gift, through faith. Once I received this amazing gift from God, I begin to wonder how someone could make it without grace. I cannot begin to imagine my life without grace, how much I need grace, and wonder how people can live so long without it.

I allowed His grace to become the motivation that I needed to move forward and to get me through each day. In my season of grief, grace became that indwelling quality that I needed within me, and the quality that I needed to help me complete each tasks that God had assigned to me. *James 4:6* (ESV), *But he gives more grace. Therefore it says, "God opposes the proud, but gives grace to the humble."*

I knew that I was going to need *more grace*; God's grace to help me through this process, so I had to humble myself each day and ask God for His grace. Many times we want to pick and choose our own assignment. Jesus never chose his assignments; he just went to where the need was, and where God sent him. He knew he was a sent one. *He who began a good work in you will bring it to completion at the day of*

Jesus Christ (Philippians 1:6 ESV), God finished the work that he needed to do through Jesus. I have great faith that God finished the work that he needed to do through my husband and is completing the work that still needs to be done through me.

I felt like Jesus when he said these words, *Father, if you are willing, please take this cup of suffering away from me, Luke 22:42 (NLV).* Then you have to think back and remember why you were called in the first place. Jesus went to the garden of Gethsemane three different times and prayed. *Matthew 26:39 (NLV), He went on a little farther and got down with His face on the ground. He prayed.* This really ministered to me; if we would take out the time to go a little further into our prayer closet, go a little deeper in prayer, and go a little longer in prayer, it would pull us closer to God. Moreover, this would allow us to get a deeper revelation, direction, and clarity from God. Each time that Jesus went to the Garden of Gethsemane to pray, He went a little further, he went beyond them. We have to go beyond the distractions and people that may interfere with our hearing from God.

Luke 22:43 (NLV), An angel from heaven came and gave Him strength. Jesus came to a place of submission and surrendered to God's will. God gave Him the grace and the strength to carry out His assignment, therefore he realized it was not His will but the will of the Father and He said: *Yet I want your will to be done, not mine.* Jesus had to drink of the cup that was assigned to Him. There are a lot of Leaders that could really benefit from a Gethsemane experience. God gave Jesus everything that He needed to carry out that assignment. God will give us the same serving grace and power to carry out every assignment. God will give us the power to do all we need to do for Him.

I needed His spirit and His power to rest upon me and in me; as it says in His Word in:

Isaiah 61:1-3 (MSG), The Spirit of God, the Master, is on me because God anointed me. He sent me to preach good news to the poor, heal the heartbroken, Announce freedom to all captives, pardon all prisoners. God sent me to announce the year of his grace—a celebration of God's destruction of our enemies—and to comfort all who mourn, To care for the needs of all who mourn in Zion, give them bouquets of roses instead of ashes, Messages of joy instead of news of doom, a praising heart instead of a languid spirit. Rename them "Oaks of Righteousness" planted by God to display his glory.

Isaiah 61:1-3 (KJV), 1The Spirit of the Lord GOD is upon me; because the LORD hath anointed me to preach good tidings unto the meek; he hath sent me to bind up the brokenhearted, to proclaim liberty to the captives, and the opening of the prison to them that are bound; 2 To proclaim the acceptable year of the LORD, and the day of vengeance of our God; to comfort all that mourn; 3 To appoint unto them that mourn in Zion, to give unto them beauty for ashes, the oil of joy for mourning, the garment of praise for the spirit of heaviness; that they might be called trees of righteousness, the planting of the Lord, that he might be glorified.

I will continue to carry out God's will. I knew that in order for God to continue to do the supernatural through me, I was going to need His divine grace.

Romans 8:28 (NIV), And we know that in all things God works for the good of those who love him, who have been called according to his purpose.

Grace is the quality that I need to carry out and fulfill the call that is upon my life. God's grace is one of the most powerful forces in the universe. It reaches you where you are and takes you where God wants you to be. Grace really took me through, even when there were times that I didn't want to nor did I feel like it, but knew that I had to. There were times that I felt that this was too much for me, but I held onto the word of God and my faith. I focus on encouraging scriptures that would assure me that God will give me strength or whatever it was that I needed to just simply make it through that day or that moment. God will strengthen us through His Word. God also sends encouragement through family, friends and other people, who hurt for you and with you. It never ceased to amaze me when that divine phone call with a scripture or a visit from a family member or close friend would take place.

When I would hurt or became extremely sad, I was honest with God and told him exactly how I was feeling at that moment. Some days I needed a lot more comforting and peace than I did on other days. I had to believe that God would give me strength and peace when I did not have any of my own. When I felt this task or journey was too much for me at times, I had to realize it wasn't too much for God. I could trust God to lead me through this season of grief and at the same time, *"Do something through me that was beyond me."* I trusted Him to give me the grace that I needed to continue to carry out the plan He had for my life. We never know how effective it is to live our life by demonstrating our faith and how helpful it can be to someone else. We have to allow ourselves to become available for God, so He can use us as a willing vessel even at times when it doesn't feel good, and allow Him to demonstrate His power through us. God continued to do *something through me that was beyond me.*

I continue to move forward with God's grace being my motivation, hoping and praying that each day will get a little easier, while allowing God's Words in scriptures to comfort me.

- ❖ *Isaiah 40:28-31 (NKJV) Have you not known? Have you not heard? The everlasting God, the Lord, the Creator of the ends of the earth, neither faints nor is weary. His understanding is unsearchable.*[29] *He gives power to the weak, And to those who have no might He increases strength.*[30] *Even the youths shall faint and be weary, And the young men shall utterly fall,*[31] *But those who wait on the LORD Shall renew their strength; They shall mount up with wings like eagles, They shall run and not be weary, They shall walk and not faint.*

- *Psalm 62:1 (NIV) My soul finds rest in God alone; my salvation comes from him.*
- Psalm 119:49-50 (NIV)[49-]Remember your word to your servant, for you have given me hope.[50] My comfort in my suffering is this: Your promise preserves my life.
- *Matthew 28:20(NIV)*[20] *... And surely I am with you always, to the very end of the age.*
- *Jeremiah 29:11 (NIV)*[11] *For I know the plans I have for you," declares the LORD, "plans to prosper you and not to harm you, plans to give you hope and a future.*
- *John 14:27 (NIV)*[27] *Peace I leave with you; my peace I give you. I do not give to you as the world gives. Do not let your hearts be troubled and do not be afraid.*

The Lord shall renew my strength. There is the old saying, "It gets worse before it gets better," well it did. I take great joy in knowing that God will renew my strength whenever my bad days come and that He will comfort me through His Word. There are times in a person's life that they may experience loss of a loved one, tragedy or situations that are out of their control. There may even be times when you may feel so alone and that you are all by yourself and that the whole world is against you. You must remember that you can always find comfort in God's Word. *Romans 8:31 (NIV), What, then, shall we say in response to these things? If God is for us, who can be against us?* God's Word reassured me that I was not alone and that He was with me as I went through my transition and season of grief.

Transition from Grief to Hope

I transitioned through my grief with the hope and the promises that are recorded in God's Word when he said in *Deuteronomy 31:6 that he would never leave me nor forsake me.*

I have learned some valuable lessons from my husband. He was wise beyond his years. I loved, respected and believed in him enough to listen to the God that was on the inside of him. He was a man of great faith. If he didn't know how to do something, he would not give up until he figured it out. "Can't hold me hostage," he would say. Then he would say, "Let me pray about it, and God will tell me what to do and the Holy Ghost will show me how to do it." We would often preach to one another and steal each other thoughts and revelation. I had to hide my notes from him at times. When the Holy Spirit would reveal something to him, he would not hold on to it for himself and apply it to just his life, or our life, but he would share it with whoever would listen and receive it from him. He was very obedient to do what God would tell to him to do.

One of the first scriptures he told me to memorize was, *Psalm 1*. He said, "When you learn this and get this down in your Spirit, it will take you a long way baby girl." Then he would shout, "GLORY!" then smile and laugh.

***Blessed is the man that walketh not in the counsel of the ungodly, nor standeth in the way of sinners, nor sitteth in the seat of the scornful. 2 But his delight is in the law of the Lord; and in his law doth he meditate day and night. 3 And he shall be like a tree planted by the rivers of water, that bringeth forth his fruit in his season; his leaf also shall not wither; and whatsoever he doeth shall prosper. 4 The ungodly are not so: but are like the chaff which the wind driveth away. 5 Therefore the ungodly shall not stand in the judgment, nor sinners in the congregation of the righteous. 6 For the Lord knoweth the way of the righteous: but the way of the ungodly shall perish.* Psalm 1:1-6 KJV**

I will forever cherish all the memories we made together. We had some good times, some rough times and some sad times, but because of the grace of God we made it through them all.

One of the things that made our marriage healthy; is that we laughed a lot. My husband loved life and was not going to waste time arguing with anyone. He would not even argue with me, he would tell me, "Tina, I'm too old to argue with you baby girl." Pastor Releford was a mighty man of God, he was a provider, giver, very forgiving Spirit, and loved to fellowship with God and all of God's people. He never met a stranger. I have hope that I will see him in Paradise.
Something Beyond me—Gods Supernatural Divine Grace; has truly been extended to me through my time of transition and grief. No matter what you may go through and experience in life, keep your heart pure and remember this scripture: *Romans 8:38-39 (NKJV),*[38] *For I am persuaded that neither death nor life, nor angels nor principalities nor powers, nor things present nor things to come,*[39] *nor height nor depth, nor any other created thing, shall be able to separate us from the love of God which is in Christ Jesus our Lord.*

I grieve with the confidence as recorded in *Psalms 34:18 The Lord is close to the brokenhearted and saves those who are crushed in Spirit.* I was brokenhearted and crush but I remain hopeful and kept my hope in God. I had to trust God in the mist of my grief. I had to lean on God in the mist of my pain. When tragedy comes in our life, there is no other comfort or peace like that of which we receive from God. In times like this we can find it difficult to hold on to hope. We have the ability to allow God's love to calm our restlessness as He whispers words of love and hope into our ears.

Whatever condition or situation we may be in, we have a **but not** to comfort us. In *2 Corinthians 4:8-9 (NIV), 8 We are hard pressed on every side,* **but not** *crushed;* We can receive help from God, *Perplexed,* **but not** *in despair;* knowing that God is able to support us and, and deliver us *9 persecuted,* **but not** *abandoned;* God will never abandoned us. *Struck down,* **but not** *destroyed.* When we are hurting or may feel wounded, the Lord will raise us up again to continue on. When difficulties and circumstances that are out of our control become unbearable and our human resources are exhausted, God's resources are given to expand our faith, hope, and strength.

Transitioning from Grief to hope with these comforting words of the Lord:

❖ *Romans 5:5 (NKJV) Now hope does not disappoint, because the love of God has been poured out in our hearts by the Holy Spirit who was given to us.*

The outpouring love of God is so amazing. I experience the outpouring love of God in my heart through the Holy Spirit during my time of grief. God's love and grace continued to sustain me during my season of grief. This hope that I have in God, *it does not disappoint.* Everyone should know what it is like to have the love of God poured out in their hearts. It is a deep, inner awareness of God and is an experience with God, especially in time of grief.

❖ *Romans 15:13 (NKJV) Now may the God of hope fill you with all joy and peace in believing, that you may abound in hope by the power of the Holy Spirit.*

God is a God of hope, He is the foundation on which hope is built, and is the object of our hope. We should desire and long for an abundance of hope. This type of hope only comes through the power of the Holy Spirit. Our own power will never reach it. The love that God pours in our heart is an ever-present experience of His love that sustains us in suffering and assures us that our hope for the future is not false. In God we can rejoice in hope. We can look beyond our present problems to a hope in God, because of the grace that God has given to us through faith.

I thank God for his everlasting love, power, and grace that he has extended to me to help me to get through this painful season in my life. There were times when my hurt and pain did not want to (spiritually) hear about the *hope* that I have in God. We must realize that we can always find peace and assurance in God's Word. God did something in me and through me that was beyond me. Glory! I will remain hopeful, *Acts 17:28* (NIV) *says: For in him we live and move and have our being.* As some of your own poets have said, 'We are his offspring.'

Something Beyond Me—God's Supernatural Divine Grace

2 Cor. 12:9 *"My grace is sufficient for you, for my power is made perfect in weakness." Therefore I will boast all the more gladly about my weaknesses, so that Christ's power may rest on you.*

Pastor Releford Inspiring Quotes:

- ❖ "You can't treat People the same way they treat you!"
- ❖ "The more God does for you the sweeter you ought to become"
- ❖ "God will treat you like you're the only child he has!"
- ❖ "There is nothing that you could ever do to make God stop loving you!"
- ❖ "Baby girl, stay out of my business!"
- ❖ "God does not hold us accountable for what we don't know, he only holds us accountable for what we do know!"
- ❖ "Heaven is a prepared place for prepared people!"
- ❖ "Nobody holds me hostage, I been doing this for a long time!"

Pastor Releford Inspiring Quotes:

- ❖ "Prayer changes things, and if you pray long enough, prayer will change you!"
- ❖ "God is a perpetual God; by the time you make your move he has already made another move!"
- ❖ "Let me and Jessie rob this train!"
- ❖ "You can't beat God!"
- ❖ "Ole Releford is cleaner than the board of health!"
- ❖ "This room isn't big enough to whoop a cat!"
- ❖ "Some things have to be caught and not taught!"
- ❖ "I got this, I got this!"
- ❖ "We are not having any dead church today!"
- ❖ "Prayer can go where you can't go!"
- ❖ "Only thing that comes to a sleeper is a dream!"
- ❖ "Spirit to Spirit Ministries... 'We're Going Somewhere!'"
- ❖ "Somebody shout glory!"
- ❖ "Eat the meat an throw the bone away."
- ❖ "Now is not the time to back up like a crawdad."

One of Pastor Releford's most powerful quotes that he would always recite to himself is:

He would look at himself in the mirror and say; *"I'm not satisfied with that man in the mirror."* That statement encouraged and became the motivation that he needed to help him work harder at becoming a better person and do better today, than he did yesterday. Striving for perfection!

About the Author

Prophetess Tina Perry Releford

God has enriched my life in so many ways that's forever changing in thriving to do His will. Prophetess Tina is very passionate about being a servant of The Lord, and is very anointed and operates in various gifts that edify the body of Christ. One of the gifts that Prophetess Tina works in the most is, deliverance.  Prophetess Tina's heart goes out to women and young girls that are in Bondage, Broken and Abandoned.

The Lord has anointed her with a strong spiritual influence to help push the people of God to another dimension in Christ; out of the Pit and into the Palace, out of Captivity to Freedom.

Proud Mother and Grandmother; Prophetess Tina became a licensed minister November 3, 2002 and an ordained Co-Pastor of *Spirit to Spirit Ministries* on June 22, 2013.

www.ingramcontent.com/pod-product-compliance
Lightning Source LLC
Chambersburg PA
CBHW051710090426
42736CB00013B/2637